Democracy's Garden of Hope

Written By:
Anne Lingelbach

Illustrated By:
Hannah Vale

Published by Orange Hat Publishing 2025
SCISBN: 9781645386377
HC ISBN: 9781645386384

Copyright © 2025 by Anne Lingelbach
All Rights Reserved
Democracy's Garden of Hope
Written by Anne Lingelbach
Illustrated by Hannah Vale

This publication and all contents within may not be reproduced or transmitted in any part or in its entirety without the written permission of the author.

OrangeHat
PUBLISHING

orangehatpublishing.com

Dedicated to our children

In a world where *freedom* and *democracy* thrive
there is *hope*.

In a world where government is *inclusive* and *accountable*
there is *hope*.

In a world where people are treated *fairly*
there is *hope*.

America's *democracy* is known as a problem-solving system. The government solves world problems, nurtures *good ideas*, addresses its citizens' concerns, and *cooperates* with allies around the world.

American democracy is a *representative* one. The people elect representatives to run the government.

In an election, the leaders who get the most votes win the election. The people must *accept the results* of an election even if their choice of leaders did not win.

The elected leaders follow the *Constitution* when making decisions. The Constitution is the highest law in America.

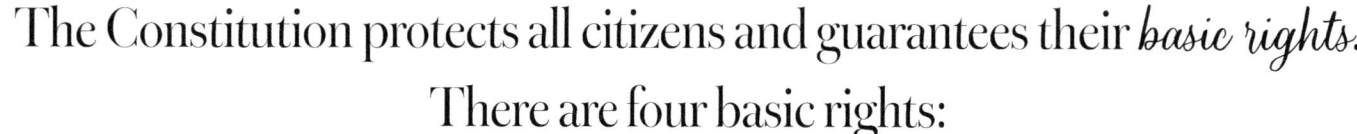

The Constitution protects all citizens and guarantees their *basic rights*.
There are four basic rights:
1. *Equality* and *justice* for everyone
2. *Free* and *fair* elections for citizens to *vote* for their leaders
3. Preservation of everyone's *individual rights*
4. *Distribution* of authority among the three branches of government

America's *democracy* must always be *protected*. A democracy is like a *flower*. To survive, it needs *strong roots* and consistent care. Each generation of Americans has a responsibility to become *gardeners* and continue the care of their democracy.

Flowers connect people to the world around them. There is a *language* of flowers which can help people to understand the world.

Flowers symbolize many different *ideals*. Some flowers symbolize attributes of a democracy like *hope*, *freedom*, *equality*, and *justice*.

Flower Poetry is a way to capture the language of flowers. The following flower poems are written in the *Lune format*. The Lune is an American haiku.

It is a three lined poem that follows a 3 word, 5 word, 3 word pattern.

Here is an example of a Lune poem.

Freesia

Trust, freedom, joy
Aromatic calming fresh citrus scent
Survives challenging times

Hydrangea

Honesty, dignity, friendship
Symbolizes community, unity and friendship
Appreciate life's blessings

Azalea

Moderation, care, balance
Caring for yourself and others
Thinking of home

Yellow Sunflower

Welcome, optimism, happiness
Flower faces follow the sun
Reduces stressful feelings

Nasturium

Patriotism, heroism, victory
Fighting courageously for one's beliefs
Promotes emotional energy

Cosmos

Balance, simplicity, serenity
Has calming influence on people
Joyful, peaceful, beauty

Red Poppy

Consolation, remembrance, death
Hope for a peaceful future
American Legion Poppy

Forget-Me-Not

Equality, friendship, respect
Symbol of true blue friends
Always remember me

Black-Eyed-Susan

Justice, encouragement, wonder
Sends messages of new beginnings
Promotes emotional energy

Dahlia

Steadfastness, commitment, kindness
Remembered for embracing positive changes
Unique showy blooms

Daffodil

Creativity, energy, rebirth
Praises the beauty of nature
Lightens up landscapes

Iris

Wisdom, faith, hope
Perseverance through life's daily challenges
Color nurtures tranquility

Lavender

Peace, renewal, healing
Offers opportunities to move forward
Fragrant, graceful, respectful

Tiger Lily

Resilience, courage, harmony
A reminder to stand tall
Embrace your uniqueness

Blue Hyacinthe

Sincerity, fidelity, constancy
I am there for you
Signals Spring's arrival

Zinnia

Strength, endurance, honor
Faith that cannot be broken
One tough cookie

Goldenrod

Fortune, encouragement, growth
Flowers can help reduce depression
Survives harsh environments

Aster

Hope, enthusiasm, fun
Never forget your inner child
Star shaped flower

www.ingramcontent.com/pod-product-compliance
Lightning Source LLC
LaVergne TN
LVHW071110070426
835507LV00005B/139